A Zoo

poems by

Nadia Wolnisty

Finishing Line Press
Georgetown, Kentucky

A Zoo

Copyright © 2018 by Nadia Wolnisty
ISBN 978-1-63534-385-4 First Edition
All rights reserved under International and Pan-American Copyright Conventions. No part of this book may be reproduced in any manner whatsoever without written permission from the publisher, except in the case of brief quotations embodied in critical articles and reviews.

ACKNOWLEDGMENTS

Ark for the Axolotl appeared in *Spry Literary Journals*, Fall 2017
Birds of Barcelona appeared in *Do Not Go Gentle,* Spring 2010
My Left Ear appeared in *University Scholar*, Fall 2012
Dead Dog Music appeared on *MadSwirl.com*
Poem for My Birthday appeared on *CommonCompany.com*
Quiet appeared in the *White Rock Zine Machine*, as a tiny zine
Owl Burying appeared in *University Scholar*, Spring 2011
Lovesong for Whale Vomit and Sadness appeared in *Apogee*, April 2017

Publisher: Leah Maines
Editor: Christen Kincaid
Cover Art: Emmy Piercy
Author Photo: Roselyn Hoang
Cover Design: Elizabeth Maines McCleavy

Printed in the USA on acid-free paper.
Order online: www.finishinglinepress.com
　　　　　　 also available on amazon.com

Author inquiries and mail orders:
Finishing Line Press
P. O. Box 1626
Georgetown, Kentucky 40324
U. S. A.

Table of Contents

Avocado with Bones 1

Ark for the Axolotl 3

Bear with Bib 5

Birds of Barcelona 7

What Rust Does 8

Bonefolder 10

My Left Ear 12

Dead Dog Music 13

Poem for my Birthday 14

On a Painting by Goya 15

Quiet 16

Owl-Burying 17

Dark Meat 19

The Urinal 21

Fear the Animals 22

No Pumice for Sarah 24

Lovesong for Whale Vomit and Sadness 26

Avocado with Bones

Alligator pears is what my father used to call them,
citing the Mexican nickname for the avocado
every time we passed them in the grocery store.

It's easy to see why. The skin a green leather
hardness over that cumbersome shape and
tendency to be ripe for two minutes only.

I don't know if that's true or not,
what the Mexicans call the fruit.
Hearing my father talk was like hearing
someone play Two Truths and a Lie,
without the guessing afterward.

*You can use the brushes along the escalators
to clean the bottom of your shoes,* he'd say,
and, *Any idiot can drive. Plenty of them do,*
and *I would never do anything to hurt you.*

Regardless of what avocado's nickname is,
I do know it's not true—that it's part alligator
and part pear. But I always wanted it to be,
because I want anything fantastical to be true.
A strange child of fruit and animal
here in the grocery store. A tendency
to fall apart along with that infamous bite.

Their jaws are what make
alligators have collectible bones.
Pears and I do not. I know this is true.
My father, he broke mine—
the one we name the tail.

An avocado I stuck in a drawer
of my fridge two weeks ago and forgot about
is miraculously ripe.
How ready, how perfect it felt,
not too firm, not too soft, like
holding the hand of someone you trusted.

I pointed the stem towards myself and examined.
It looked like a jut of bone. I flicked
it with my thumbs. It came right off.

I know that they say who ever gets
the fat part of the wishbone when it breaks
gets their wish. I don't know
what they say about avocado bones.
Perhaps it means it's my turn
to play Two Truths and a Lie.

I forgive you, I forgive you, I forgive you.

Ark for the Axolotl

Remember the axolotl and her anxiety,
because when Noah got to Mexico,
with his wife, kids, and net,
Noah saw her front paw budding anew with blood
and thought just one will work when it's time.

Remember the axolotl when she saw
all the other animals gracefully
entwined. Even the box turtles
turned spritely, with eight sets of toes
sticking out like exclamation points,
the two giraffes with necks wended into hearts.

And she wondered what shape her story would be,
with thighs eggless, mateless. An open
parenthesis ellipses close parenthesis,
perhaps. Nothing inside but the hope that
things will work when it's time and the worry
that for his disobedience, Noah might be remiss.

Carriage for water. Barge. Boat. Ship.
She won't use the word *ark*,
because *ark* sounds like *arc*,
and what if there is no shape for this story?
What if things won't work when it's time?

And the axolotl's anxiety must've been like
squatting in a bathroom stall under fluorescents,
blood and tissue in clumps between thighs,
then exiting through an elevator and cold autumn
to a doctor who says these things happen
sometimes. Things'll work when it's time.

For now, the axolotl watches the others
urgently courting. She'll wait for dry land
to be close by before rending herself in half
and regrowing each half—trying to, at least.
(What if things don't work when it's time?)
Her smile is secretly a grimace,
her eyes reflect black like the storm.

Bear with Bib

You had a bear, and it scared me.
Blue bib stitched on front and missing fur.
Panda from your infancy and my nightmares.
You loved it into destruction, taking
it with you into our overgrown backyard.
All our games had to have Bibby—
so named because our mother had sewn a patch
on the front where you had ripped it open.

I obliged you. You were two years younger
than I, and I needed to show everyone
how kind and mature I was.
I wouldn't touch it though.
We played outside most days
until our father came home.
When we heard his car pull in the driveway,
we ran inside. We pretended not to know why.

But many times, you would forget
which corner of the yard you left
your soft bear, and we would sneak out later to find him.
I wished he would leave—climb on the chairs
and over the wall, like I did, years later,
to sneak cigarettes at night.
That bear was hideous, useless, thin.

You, too, keep getting thinner,
and I am afraid of your thinness.
No one will sew patches on you,
and replace what has leaked out.
You don't have enough mass to hold
yourself up. I dream you are a beanpole,
which is what our father called you—
bodies common property for comment
and consumption. Loving us into destruction.

You had x-ray done for where an old rip
is in your lumbar. You said you didn't
know where it came from, and when I obliged you,
I felt like I had polyester inside my lungs.

I want to find you that bear—the one with the blue bib.
It's twenty-five years old and long gone.
But know that if I did find it, I would be kind to it.
I would love it without flinching.

Birds of Barcelona

You told me about birds,
why if you tie magnets to their feet
and drive them in your car
they can't find their way home,

and how in Barcelona
the pigeons, wrens, and gulls flock together
and to be sure to buy seed while there.

You told me about birds,
why they can't be held
even if they perch on your shoulder,
about bones being brittle
to keep things hollow
for flight.

What Rust Does

Look at how beautiful this rust is.
It is the color of your beard or
the leaves in fall where you're from.

The butterfly is credited with
metamorphosis and flight,
but rust does both and better.
It is both the act of transubstantiation
and the end result. A gust of wind
allows it to fly everywhere all
at once, like my fingers scratching
your back in circles
to help you fall asleep.

What I was a kid, I was told
to keep everything locked up tight.
Make your hand into a fist and put it
over your heart. That is the size of it.

My parents' backyard gate had the lock
on the inside, I had to reach over it
on my toes and fumble with a key.
One year, the lock rusted out,
and the gate swung freely,
back and forth, like hands
beckoning *Come in, Come in.*

I had tried to write a poem
about how much you mean,
but wrote about trash and tetanus instead.
Forgive me, I am a little rusty.

The first draft of this poem was called
Intimacy and was three lines only,
a series of diminishing screams:
Ahhhhhhh.
Ahhhh.
Ahhh.

But what I really want to say is:
I like waking up next to you,
splayed over more than my half of the bed,
out like two palms open in thanksgiving.

Once, I managed to wake up
before you did, and I walked out in my backyard.
I was in my bare feet, the way you warned me not to.
The sun was red, orange. I almost stepped on a nail.
I reached down and placed it
between both palms as if it were communion.
Something for mere utility was growing bark.
Something sharp was being made a tree.

Bonefolder

It only sounds terrifying.
Like a Medieval torture device
or something in a slaughterhouse
on an industrial chicken-farm.

But the bonefolder is a tool for making books—
and a simple one, at that. It felt
so familiar when I held one, for the first time
like an old friend, or something I
had as a child,
like a crib or pacifier,
since the corners are rounded
the way things for infants always are.

It was about eight inches
by one inch by the thickness of a toenail.
The old ones were made of bone, presumably.
Mine was plastic, but still smooth and cool.
It reminded me of a rib on a folding fan
my grandmother used to have.
We picked the peacock feathers off after she died.

To use, I run it along the fold
to make that edge as sharp as I can.
I must be swift. I must be certain.
Then, I press it over the pages
to get the wrinkles out.

Losses, too, sound terrifying,
like something that will make me weak
or, worse, grotesque and easy to consume.

But they will feel familiar, like
something I've always held
from before I could even remember.
Cool and smooth.

I never quite got the hang of it, though;
how to use a loss like a bonefolder.
I must be swift, I must be certain.
I want what I've lost to act as a bonefolder
and help smooth out my wrinkles.
My edges sharp so that I, too,
can be a neat little book of my own making.

But what edges I do have from losses,
are ragged like my toenails
I bite off when they get too long and they
always catch me by surprise—
losses are small hooks,
growing on the ends of me.

My Left Ear

A crustacean has taken up residence in my left ear. I am unsure of its species, as it is very small and never pokes its head out of its newfound shell. It has dozens of legs, and perhaps an expert could use them to identify it. The legs are long and spindly and quiver constantly. I know this because I see them when I shave in the morning.

At lunch, when Ms. Anderson was saying how she was afraid to have children because her mother had three stillborns and was that sort of thing hereditary and Mrs. Jones was telling something about her ex-husband, Ms. Anderson coughed pointedly behind her napkin. Mrs. Jones looked up from her menu and screeched at me. Embarrassed, I left without paying the bill or collecting my coat.

Evicting it would be a simple matter with tweezers and a mirror, but I find myself reluctant, despite having to take my meals at home. The crustacean would be undoubtedly helpless, and assuming it found a new habitat, suppose it was less hospitable? Besides, I would no longer have an excuse to decline invitations, and my hearing of divorce, inheritance disputes, and the weather would be unimpeded.

My right ear is quite unoccupied, thank God, because then it would all be over. If another crustacean should lodge itself, next snails would move into each nostril, and two bats would hang on either side of my uvula. I would be but a little ark in a flood of tears.

Dead Dog Music

Your music sounds like roadkill,
I told you when we first met.
Perhaps you didn't hear me or were a little offended,
because you got quiet.

But I figured this was an okay thing to say
because you had asked me, quite blankly,
if I had ever installed dry wall and if
I had enjoyed inhaling and then coughing up the particles.
I told you *No*, with all the dignity I could muster,
but was thinking *Dear god, that sounds amazing*
and *I want to.*

What I meant, though, was
it's the music of the real, and
that can be jarring sometimes
and cause for pause—like seeing matted fur
outside your car window.

Roadkill isn't like other rubbish; you can't
just pick it up and throw it away
or use a bottle when your ashtray gets full.
There is a particular resilience to roadkill,
even after the damage has been done.

I don't know what the roadkill is like
over in New York where you are
learning to dance quietly
like the end of a fishing pole,
where you are learning about how small
a house can be, and how to leave the few
safe places you have known.

Perhaps there's more squirrels,
less dogs, more birds, or some big elk.
But I think if you make music like
the flash of fur and red through a window
then the cruelty of heavy things
won't ever make you frail.

Poem for My Birthday

The gruesome beauty of childhood
does not translate well past the age of twenty-two.
That feeling you got upon finding
an old doll, broken, missing an arm,

the dog bite intricate impression on plastic.
You had called her Princess Falafel
because you liked the sound of it,
and that day, she promoted herself to Queen.

Or when you had to stare at green,
post-nuclear soup for hours, after
the grown-ups said it was split-pea
—the pink ham appalling cubed flesh—

and you refused to eat it
because it reeked of what it was before
and you went to bed hungry
but triumphant for not relenting.

Re-found, broken things won't cut into you
anymore because you're biggest prime number you know,
you've already ordered the replacement,
and you will never be forced to stare it down.

Late April in Texas, the air is like porridge
in hair and mouth and clothes.
You feel so full from breathing,
you won't have to eat for years.

On a Painting by Goya

I.

We thought the painting was Satan Devouring his Son.
Dad said that wasn't in the bible,
which explained why we didn't know it.
He said, *Satan didn't have any children.*
We said, *Of course not, not anymore,*
he ate them.

The blackness in the background,
different kinds of nothing, must have been hell.
There wasn't any fires in this part, we supposed,
just something letting us see
demon flesh clutching the flesh it made.

I felt sorry for them, father and son both,
to be caught up in so much motion.
The son with his arm raised in protest,
back caving in like a hot game-hen,
to be used so entirely by one person.

The father, too, shaggy hair in swing from
the jerk back, to have eyes flat and startled,
with eyebrows raised as if embarrassed
to be caught in a moment so candid.

II.

At school, we learned of Rama and Ra,
Apollo and Aeneas and all the rest.
We learned the stories of creation,
that if you want to start a cosmos,
first you have to pretend to be a stone.

Quiet

You said you liked their nightliness,
and I pictured a butterfly wearing a sweater
or something trapped and futile
like the early astronauts attempting the moon—
turning into powder somewhere along the way.

But you said they were green (bright green)
the giant lunar moths,
and mornings they would cover
your parents' garage like shingles that were alive.

I had forgotten that colors could exist at night,
even though I know colors don't stop
when things go quiet;
you just have to remember that they're there—
the orange cat is still a clumsy tiger,
the red couch still hideous and off-putting.

We stayed up all night once,
through the quiet,
so we could both be there
for what was there all along.
Soft, mauve fog rolled in, but
through the clouds, something yellow poked
like eclosion, like the calmest surprise.

Owl-Burying

We buried the body.
We bore the weight
of feathers and mice inside.

First, there was the brushing
of dirt and the wings
where they met. We separated
them with our fingertips,
careful not to disturb.

Then, you dug a hole
at the stump of an oak,
making your hands into spoons,
feeling the earth, and twigs,
and leaves that turned
into moths from the rain.

You told me to take hold
of it by the shoulder blades,
and I did, pinching lightly.
You cusped the feet.

We put it in the hole,
face up, eyes open still,
despite the cobwebs forming
in both corners.

Finally, there was the piling
of dirt back to where
it almost had been.

You began to crack
your knuckles, still hunched.
Well? you asked, and all I
could think was *Pinioned*.

We buried the body,
and I bore the weight of language
that flies with it, and my mouth
felt like I had eaten
spoonfuls of moths.

Dark Meat

I.

I thought it dark and unholy,
but no great mystery. My father
had told me because I had asked
what the casing of sausage was
made of. *It isn't plastic*, he said,
*so it's safe to eat. It's actually
a little gross. It's the lining of
the pig's small intestine, since
it's already an almost perfect
tube. Well,* I said, *what's it
stuffed with?* And my father
said, *You don't want to know.*
So I assumed it was shit.

Well, not shit, shit. But the
unusable part that even a pig
wouldn't digest but had not
passed yet. I felt a little
queasy with the knowing
but soon got over it, like
Adam and Eve after they knew
about distinctions but didn't stop.

And I didn't stop either,
that's the oddest part. I ate
the bratwursts on The Fourth,
sweaty and vulgar, the patties
at special breakfasts, held to-
gether by gravity and intention.

I, too, was held together by
gravity and intention. It was
unholy what they did to me,
but no great mystery. I was

not made of plastic; I couldn't
bend, and they made the worst
guesses for what was inside

Now, two decades later,
I see beauty in my ridiculous
belief that sausages are made
out of unpassed shit (which
is somehow different than
shit shit). It's the unerring
hope that even what is
unfathomably worthless
can take on a second life.

II.

You made me chorizo for
breakfast the morning after,
with onions, tortillas, eggs
too runny because that's
how I like them. *Don't
read the ingredients on the
package,* you said.
Don't worry, I won't.

The Urinal

In late September, the clouds empty their bladders
in warm tinkles. Their streams coalesce in a large ashtray
on top of a trash can outside of my work.
The cigarette-butts develop rectal prolapse ,
and distend themselves, and form the worst soup.

I stand like a broken kite, my shoe filling up with blood.
I had stepped on a sliver of broken wineglass the day before,
and it stuck stubbornly half in, half out.
I wondered if you could die that way, a piece of glass
sailing towards the heart.

I put out my cigarette out in the corner of the ashtray
where a spider is forming its web.
I am an arsonist in miniature. The silk tendrils
curl into themselves like nervous fingers.
The spider scrambles in silent alarm,
front arms out in dismay.
My home, my home.
It was a terrible place to live anyways.

Fear the Animals
    for A.E.

I.

We feared the animals leaving,
but always we knew what to say
with each passing.

When the honeybees fell mid-flight,
we said *The scientists, the activists,*
they were right. Something to do
with the pollutants, the pesticides mostly.

And we knew what we would tell our children
if they ever saw pictures in history books.
The helicopter-flies. They danced back and forth
and made a golden syrup of spun flower
to make our food palatable.

Same with the last polar bear.
Oh, we tried, we tried.
The icecaps outraced evolution, and
we couldn't teach anything how to win.
The last one, a male, we think, died in a Coca-Cola zoo,
thin, patchy, like a thrift-store sweater.

We said to the children: *We'll take you*
to the tomb some day, if it's still open.
The stone says the bear's dates and name: Majestic.

II.

But when the waterbears went,
the tardigrades, the moss-pigs,
we didn't know what we would say.

All over the globe,
even the ones we shot into space,
they just curled up like fists one morning,
as if they all vomited tiny universes.

The scientists were calm, at first,
hoping that the waterbears were hibernating,
because that is what survivors do,
and that they would come back,
with eight spiny limbs bursting,
shouting *Surprise, surprise.*

But the bodies began to decay,
flakes floating in grotesque arabesques.
We saw grainy videos of them dissolving
and thought that music ought to play.

Because if they can't, then we can't.
We aren't built for whatever is coming.
We need cars, and can-openers, and
and a series of descending shelters:
atmosphere, home, clothes.
Pills to sleep, and when we dream,
it gives off radiation.

And when one of our own dies,
we spend all night in a shitty apartment
full of vodka and grown men crying
because he was dead,
and there was nothing else we could do.

Tardigrades need none of those things,
not even air, and lead simple lives,
barely noticeable, gathering fuel.
What to tell the children of their passing?

Because it felt like if they can't do it, then we can't.
Our armor isn't made for pesticide and zoos
or outer-space or oceans or desert, and our armor is
more flimsy than flowers or water.
     ….And yet, reader, here we are.

No Pumice for Sarah

I.
The end of the world won't be a big hole,
but a series of small ones.
Think of a piece of wood that the termites
got into, leaving everything lattice-work
and saliva-filled lace.

It will start with you, start with your skin
like acne scars without the acne first.
When holes get bigger, there's less of them.
Your body with look like the pictures we found
in our parents' Encyclopedia Britannica
of blood vessels, but covered in muscle and skin,
trying still to hold.

Next, it will be the ground you're on.
Eaten by acid, almost. Asphalt will resemble
ash the moment before it disintegrates—
dirt will be churned as if by a universal harvester,
concrete like a paper target
hit by the smallest, most imprecise of guns.

II.

Your birth was the beginning of spring
and my earliest of memories.
I went to the hospital in my pajamas when
you were born. I think this means
you will see the end.

You said that would be
your worst nightmare,
if everything were a web of holes,

peering up like lidless eyes.
You've avoided pumice, loofas,
cheese graters for twenty-five years
so successfully, so carefully.

And if the world ends in small holes,
I think you'll be alright,
despite your phobia. You grew up
in a home where you had to balance
on lattice-work spread out like blood vessels.
It was the most holes I've seen in one place.

And if everything does become
perforated like park benches,
you can balance an egg on its small end,
and not just on your birthday.

Note: There is a Medieval belief that an egg can balance on its small end during the Spring Solstice.

Lovesong for Whale Vomit and Sadness

I wouldn't know it if I happened upon it
on a beach somewhere.
I would think *A petrified brain of a beast
too large to go on living, perhaps.*
Or *A rock for a fortune-teller to rub
like phrenology of the uninhabitable.*

But I would be wrong on both guesses.
Ambergris is from the gut not the head
and is worth a fortune if you find it—
smelly, hermetic, cold.

It smells of sea and fecal matter
a rock of self and environment
flung from the whale's mouth
out of—what? Irritation? A deep-
seated longing to scatter what one
can carry no more.

I tell myself depression is like ambergris.
It starts in the gut. If someone finds it,
they might not know what they are looking at.
A monstrous brain, a cryptic portent.
But after the flinging
(a body that's gotten too large contorting on carpet)
ambergris becomes essential for those who know
what it's for: a fixative for perfume,
what holds the sweetness together, when things start to shake.

Nadia Wolnisty graduated from University of Dallas, with a degree in English. Her temperament is ill-suited to academia, so it is a wonder she got by. Her favorite hobbies are observing and daydreaming. She turns her daydreams and observations into essays, line-drawings, and poetry, which has appeared in in *MadSwirl.Com*, *Apogee*, *Spry*, *Haggard and Halloo*, *Essay Daily*, *White Rock Zine Machine*, *Do Not Go Gentle*, *University Scholar*, *My Favorite Bullet*, *Grubstreet Grackle*, and the Art Uprising anthology *Desolate Country*. Her debut chapbook *Manual* was published 2017 by Cringe-Worthy Poets, who also published her line illustrations for James Barrett Rodehaver's chapbook *Time Travel for Daydreamers vol. 1 and 2*.

Surprisingly, she is deeply afraid of animals, not in the absolute sense, but more in an abstract sort of way. The idea of an intelligence so unlike our own is uncanny to her. Spiders, axolotls, bears, and tardigrades all know things in a spider, axolotl, bear, and tardigrade sort of way. How marvelous! How upsetting! How like and not-like us that is!

When she's not contemplating animals, Nadia can be found performing around Dallas. She has read with Mad Swirl (an international open mic), Poets on X+, Pegasus, Bonehouse, Common Company, and Stone Soup. She is a founding member of two workshops, Lizard Circus Family Workshop and Poetry Jacket.

She runs an artist's residence Farm Farm: Adult Orphanage in Duncanville, TX, where she lives with another poet, potter, and large, orange tom cat, whom she eyes cautiously.

www.ingramcontent.com/pod-product-compliance
Lightning Source LLC
LaVergne TN
LVHW041518070426
835507LV00012B/1668